Rent Book

Landlord: ______

I0419845

Contact: ______________________

____

____

Tenant: ______________________

Property: ______________________

____

____

Rent £ per		
Due date	Amount paid	Received by

Rent £	per	
Due date	Amount paid	Received by

Rent £	per	
Due date	Amount paid	Received by

Rent £	per	
Due date	Amount paid	Received by

Rent £	per	
Due date	Amount paid	Received by

Rent £ per		
Due date	Amount paid	Received by

Rent £	per	
Due date	Amount paid	Received by

Rent £	per	
Due date	Amount paid	Received by

Rent £	per	
Due date	Amount paid	Received by

Rent £	per	
Due date	Amount paid	Received by

Rent £	per	
Due date	Amount paid	Received by

Rent £	per	
Due date	Amount paid	Received by

Rent £	per	
Due date	Amount paid	Received by

Rent £	per	
Due date	Amount paid	Received by

Rent £	per	
Due date	Amount paid	Received by

Rent £	per	
Due date	Amount paid	Received by

Rent £	per	
Due date	Amount paid	Received by

Rent £	per	
Due date	Amount paid	Received by

Rent £	per	
Due date	Amount paid	Received by

Rent £ per		
Due date	Amount paid	Received by

Rent £ per		
Due date	Amount paid	Received by

Rent £	per	
Due date	Amount paid	Received by

www.ingramcontent.com/pod-product-compliance
Lightning Source LLC
Chambersburg PA
CBHW061953280526
45787CB00004B/1845
* 9 7 8 1 5 1 7 5 8 3 3 5 4 *